Explaining Binding And Loosing

Tom Marshall

Sovereign World

Bible quotations marked NIV are taken from
The Holy Bible, New International Version.
© Copyright 1973, 1978, 1984 International Bible Society.
Published by Hodder & Stoughton.

ISBN: 1 85240 074 9

SOVEREIGN WORLD LIMITED
P.O. Box 777, Tonbridge, Kent TN11 9XT, England.

Typeset and printed in the UK by Sussex Litho Ltd, Chichester, West Sussex.

Contents

Contents

Introduction

How to make truth real

In order to convert the spiritual truth we hear or read into actual living experience, we need to find answers to the following important questions:

1. What does it actually mean?
2. How do you do it?

If our understanding as to what the truth really means is confused or defective—
We will always have problems in obeying it, or trying to make use of it.

If we are unclear as to what is actually involved in obeying the truth or appropriating it—
Our best endeavours to translate belief into action are likely to miss the mark.

The lack of clear answers to the two questions is one of the main reasons for the huge gap that often exists between the truth we confess with our lips and the truth we experience as an on-going reality in our lives.

In the pages that follow we will try to address the same two important questions in relation to the subject of binding and loosing.

1

Binding And Loosing—
Understanding The Terms

Binding

The simplest and most straightforward meaning of the term
binding, is 'tying up'. In this sense it is used of shackling a
prisoner (Acts 12:6) or bandaging a person's wounds (Luke
10:35).

In a broader and more encompassing sense however,
binding and related words like *bonds* and *bondage*, can be
defined as:

> Restricting a person or persons in their freedom of
> action, choice or expression, or robbing them of their
> freedom, short of actual death.

Some of the words used in the New Testament to express
the same, or similar meanings, are:

> *Restrain:* The restrainer is the Holy Spirit (2 Thessal-
> onians 2:16–17).

> *Hinder:* The people responsible are the Jews (1 Thes-
> salonians 2:16).

> *Thwart* or *stop:* The agent is Satan (1 Thessalonians
> 2:18, ASB).

> *Prevent:* The factor is circumstances (Romans 1:13).

Entangle: The corruption of the world is in view (2 Peter 2:20).

Trap: The devil is the danger (2 Timothy 2:26).

Loosing

The basic meaning of *loosing* is 'untying', for example, untethering an animal (Matthew 21:2) or unwinding grave-clothes (John 11:44), but it also has the more important significance of:

Release: The object of release is the captive (Luke 4:18).

Set free: Healing from a sickness (Luke 13:16).

Cancel or *Forgive:* The remission of debts (Luke 7:42, Matthew 6:12).

Destroy a barrier: Discrimination between Jew and Gentile (Ephesians 2:14).

Permit: Allow freedom of speech (Acts 21:39–40).

Liberate: Creation freed from its bondage to corruption (Romans 8:21).

Thus we can define loosing as—

Freeing a person or persons from circumstances, people or things that restrict their freedom of action, choice or expression, or rob them of their freedom.

The Bible passages

There are three main passages that are crucial for understanding what is meant by binding and loosing. The longest and most important is Matthew 16:13–20, the others are Matthew 18:15–19 and John 20:19–20.

In discussing the practical application of binding and loosing the key passages are Matthew 12:25–30 (and its parallel Mark 3:22–27) and Luke 11:14–26.

When Jesus came to the region of Ceasarea Philippi, he asked his disciples, 'Who do people say the Son of Man is?' They replied, 'Some say John the Baptist; others say Elijah; and still others Jeremiah or one of the prophets.'

'But what about you?' he asked. 'Who do you say I am?'

Simon Peter answered, 'You are the Christ, the Son of the Living God.'

Jesus replied, 'Blessed are you, Simon son of Jonah, for this was not revealed to you by man, but by my Father in heaven. And I tell you that you are Peter, and on this rock I will build my church, and the gates of Hades will not overcome it.

I will give you the keys of the kingdom of heaven; whatever you bind on earth will be (margin 'will have been') *bound in heaven, and whatever you loose on earth will be* (margin 'will have been') *loosed in heaven'.*   (Matthew 16:13–20)

Then he warned his disciples not to tell anyone that he was the Christ.

There are several very important issues dealt with in this passage that are essential for understanding the final statement of Jesus about binding and loosing.

1. The identity of Jesus

The passage begins with Jesus introducing the subject of his identity and ends with a warning to the disciples not to make that identity public for the present. The whole passage therefore hinges on who Jesus is. There were two possibilities.

a. The Messiah; the Christ
The Hebrew word Messiah corresponds to the Greek Christos, both signifying Anointed.

Through the collapse of Israel's national dreams and aspirations the Old Testament prophets began to discern an ultimate restoration far more glorious and extensive than the nation's wildest hopes, the coming of the Messianic age and the reign of the Lord's Anointed, the Son of David.

> *Of the increase of his government and peace there will be no end. He will reign on David's throne and over his kingdom, establishing and upholding it with justice and righteousness from that time on and forever.*
>
> (Isaiah 9:7)

The prophets stretched the capacity of language to express their vision of that coming age. The wolf would live with the lamb, the infant would play near the cobra's hole. Men would beat their swords into plowshares, their spears into pruning hooks, and the nations would train for war no more.

> *They will neither harm or destroy on all my holy mountain, for the earth will be full of the knowledge of the Lord as the waters cover the sea.* (Isaiah 11:9)

b. The Prophet like Moses; the Suffering Servant
The prophets saw clearly, however, that if the Kingdom came in its holiness, it would confirm everything in harmony with it but it would destroy everything not in harmony with its holiness. They spoke of men crawling into holes in the ground and calling on the rocks to cover them from the

'great and terrible day of the Lord'. They were also speaking about the coming of the Messianic age.

But in struggling with the tension of the coming Kingdom and the fate of sinners, they saw the emergence of another figure, the prophet-like Moses (Deuteronomy 18:18), the Suffering Servant, who would take up our infirmities and carry our sorrows, whose life would be made a guilt offering and who would justify many because he would bear their iniquity (Isaiah 53:1–12).

The Jews of Jesus' day thought that these were two different persons. When John the Baptist confessed freely, *'I am not the Christ'*, the question was, *'Are you the Prophet?'* (John 1:20–21). With Jesus himself there was an on-going controversy as to whether he was the Christ or the Prophet (John 4:29, 6:14).

John the Baptist's first revelation concerning Jesus was that he was the Suffering Servant, the Lamb of God, who takes away the sin of the world (John 1:29). Only later in prison, when he heard of the miraculous works of Jesus, did he begin to think that he could also be the Messiah (Matthew 11:7).

Peter's revelation, on the other hand, was that Jesus of Nazareth was the Messiah, the Christ, the Lord's Anointed King (Matthew 16:16). Later, when Jesus began to explain that he was also the Suffering Servant, Peter had serious problems with accepting that revelation (Matthew 16:22).

Point 1. Jesus of Nazareth is the Christ, the Messiah, the Lord's Anointed King of the Kingdom of God.

2. The Rock

Because Peter is moving in revelation knowledge, Jesus takes him a step further into truth. The controversy that has surrounded the question of Peter and the rock disappears if we balance the statements made by Jesus and Peter about each other.

You are—	You are—
Peter	the Christ
the son of Jonah	the Son of the living God
Peter (petros, a stone)	the Rock (petra, mass of rock)

Moreover, the meaning would be abundantly clear to the disciples because The Rock was one of the very well known names of God in the Old Testament (Deuteronomy 32:13,15,18,30; 1 Samuel 2:2; 2 Samuel 22:2, 23:3; Psalm 18:31; Isaiah 26:4, 30:29; Habakkuk 1:12).

> *I will proclaim the name of the Lord.*
> *Oh, praise the greatness of our God!*
> *He is the Rock, his works are perfect,*
> *And all his ways are just.* (Deuteronomy 32:4)

Furthermore, Paul, looking back to the wilderness experiences when Moses brought water out of the rock (Exodus 17:6; Numbers 20:8), declares unequivocally *'that rock was Christ'* (1 Corinthians 10:4).

Point 2. Jesus of Nazareth is not only the Messiah King, he is the Rock of Israel, that is, God in Person and the foundation and builder of the church.

3. The gates of Hades

Hades is the place of departed spirits and is here spoken of as the city of death. Death and Hades always go together, even to the final judgement in the lake of fire (Revelation 1:18, 6:8, 20:13–14).

In ancient times the gates of the city were not only the means of entry and access but also the strategic key for conquering or controlling the city. Thus a person who is dying is said to *'draw near to the gates of death'* (Psalm 107:13) and capturing the city is *'possessing the gates of your enemies'* (Genesis 22:17, ASB).

Because of their strength and importance, the gates represent the power of the city. Thus the gates of Hades are *'the powers of death'* (RSV), *'the powers of the unseen'* (Con.Lit.), *'the forces of death'* (Mft) or the kingdom of death.

Point 3. Jesus Christ, the Rock of Israel, the Messianic King of the Kingdom of God is the foundation of the church, and is victorious over the strongest powers of the unseen realm, the kingdom of death itself.

4. The keys of the Kingdom

Note that the Kingdom of Heaven and the Kingdom of God are expressions meaning the same thing, the reign or rule of God. (Compare Matthew 13:30–31 with Mark 4:30–32 and Matthew 4:7 with Mark 1:15.) Matthew uses the rabbinical term in which heaven is a roundabout way of saying God.

In Scripture, the key is the symbol of authority. Thus Jesus is spoken of as having,

a. *The keys of death and hell* (Revelation 1:17–18), that is, authority over death and hell.

b. *The key of David* (Revelation 3:7, see Isaiah 22:20–23), that is, *the key or authority of the Kingdom*, he opens and no one shuts, he shuts and no one opens.

The keys of the Kingdom are the authority to exercise the power of the Kingdom to bring to pass on earth the kind of effects that take place in heaven. It means putting into effect what is expressed in the Lord's prayer.

> *Your Kingdom come,*
> *Your will be done on earth as it is in heaven*
> (Matthew 6:10).

The keys lock heaven and earth together in power to accomplish that result.

Point 4. Jesus, the Messianic King, the Rock of Israel, gives to his disciples the authority of the Kingdom, to bring the reign and rule of God to pass, on earth as it is in heaven.

5. Binding and loosing

The means whereby this accomplishing of God's rule on earth is to be achieved, is by *binding and loosing*. That is, *by restricting on earth those things that are restricted or restrained in heaven and by liberating or setting free on earth those things that are set free in heaven*. Thus earth follows heaven, and heaven dictates the course of action on earth. What this involves will come clearer as we go on.

Matthew 18:15–19

The larger context of this passage occupies the whole of chapter 18 and its setting in that chapter is the key to understanding verses 15 to 19.

The chief topic is again the Kingdom of God. It begins with the question of the disciples as to who is the greatest in the Kingdom. Jesus answers by calling a child to him and speaking about:

- Becoming a child to enter the kingdom (v 3).
- Humbling oneself like a child to be the greatest in the kingdom (v 4).
- Welcoming a child is welcoming the King of the kingdom (v 5).

Then the child (Gk paidon) becomes a symbol for all the little ones (Gk micros), that is, all those who are small or little in age, situation, rank or reputation—the humble folk and the new believers. Jesus speaks about

- Causing a little one to stumble (v 6).
- Looking down on the little ones (v 7).
- Seeking for the little one gone astray, the lost sheep (vs 10–14).

Immediately after the parable of the lost sheep, Jesus goes on to say:

> *If your brother sins against you, go and show him his fault, just between the two of you. If he listens to you, you have won your brother over. But if he will not listen, take one or two others along, so that 'every matter may be established by the testimony of two or three witnesses.' If he refuses to listen to them, tell it to the church; and if he refuses to listen even to the church, treat him as you would a pagan or a tax collector.*
>
> *I tell you the truth, whatever you bind on earth will be* (margin—will have been) *bound in heaven, and whatever you loose on earth will be* (margin—will have been) *loosed in heaven.*
>
> *Again I tell you that if two of you agree about anything you ask for, it will be done for you by my Father in heaven. For where two or three come together in my name, there am I with them.*

Here are the important points in understanding this passage.

1. *The primary aim is the winning over and recovery of the sinning brother who is a sheep that has gone astray.*

If unity and concord are restored, earth comes into harmony with heaven and whatever is asked for will be granted. It will be granted because the request will be precisely for those kind of things that are approved in heaven.

2. If the individual approach to reconciliation fails, the sinning brother is not to be abandoned but sought by means of corporate counsel from two or three together, or failing that by the church as a whole.

This is because when two or three gather in the Name of Christ, they represent his authority and secure the presence amongst them of the Lord of heaven, the King of the kingdom.

3. If the final approach fails, the sinning brother is to be treated as a pagan or a tax collector. Note that this does not mean that he is to be shunned or ostracised, because Jesus was a friend of tax gatherers and sinners and Matthew himself was once one of them.

Nor does it mean withholding forgiveness because Jesus goes on to tell the parable of the unmerciful servant to show the longsuffering nature of true forgiveness.

It means however that the offender has separated himself from the community of faith and while he remains the object of evangelism and intercession, he is no longer the object of fellowship within the body.

4. In this context binding and loosing becomes a matter of church discipline, but discipline must be exercised not out of personal hurt or grievance but in the authority of the Kingdom of God and therefore on the basis of what the Kingdom allows and what the Kingdom forbids.

Moreover the first application of binding and loosing should be redemptive, that is restricting or restraining the influences that make for strife and division and releasing the affected parties from those influences or circumstances so that reconciliation may be achieved.

The words bind and loose are not used as such in this passage, but forgive and retain are common synonyms for loose and bind when used of either money debts or moral debts or obligations (Matthew 6:12, 18:27; Romans 1:14).

> *On the evening of that first day of the week, when the disciples were together, with the doors locked for fear of the Jews, Jesus came and stood among them and said, 'Peace be with you.' After he said this, he showed them his hands and side. The disciples were overjoyed when they saw the Lord. Again Jesus said, 'Peace be with you! As the Father has sent me, I am sending you.' And with that he breathed on them and said, 'Receive the Holy Spirit. If you forgive anyone his sins, they are forgiven; if you do not forgive them, they are not forgiven.'*

There is the same sequence of authorisation and empowering here as in the previous passages, but here heaven and earth are held together by the presence of the One who holds the keys of the Kingdom. The two or three are gathered and Jesus is in their midst.

1. Authorisation
'As the Father has sent me, I am sending you' (v 21). Just as the Father gave authority to the Son (John 5:27) so now the Son gives his authority to the disciples.

2. Empowering
'Receive the Holy Spirit' (v 22). In the life and ministry of Jesus the Holy Spirit was the 'power of the Lord' (Luke 5:17). Access to the same power is now given to the disciples by the presence of the same Holy Spirit.

3. Application

The ASB translation (margin) echoes that of Matthew 16 and Matthew 18.

> *If you forgive the sins of any, their sins have previously been forgiven them; if you retain the sins of any, they have previously been retained.*

When the keys of the Kingdom lock together earth and heaven (the unseen spiritual dimension of reality where Christ reigns and the Kingdom functions in fullness) (Ephesians 1:19–23):

- The decisions of earth follow the decisions of heaven.
- The activities of earth follow the activities of heaven.
- The judgements of earth follow the judgements of heaven.
- The declarations of earth follow the declarations of heaven.

In all these situations the will and purposes of God are paramount and the Holy Spirit is the revealer of that will and those purposes.

Summary of the biblical passages

The Church has been given authority (the keys of the kingdom) and is empowered by the Holy Spirit to bring into being on earth the conditions that apply in heaven, that is accomplishing the will of God on earth as it is in heaven. The scope of this authority extends to:

Binding and loosing (Matthew 16:13–20) demons, sickness and circumstances

Binding and loosing (Matthew 18:15–19) behaviour, church discipline

Forgiving and retaining (John 20:19–23) sins.

2

The Scope of
Binding and Loosing

In Chapter 1 we defined binding and loosing as restricting freedom of action on the one hand, and releasing from such restrictions on the other.

Firstly note that binding, or bringing into bondage, is bad when a person is bound by demons or sickness or debt. But it is good when a person feels bound to keep a promise or when it means restricting the freedom of evil spirits or evil men.

Loosing is good when it means releasing someone from their fears or addictions or from demonisation, but it is bad when it means letting our mouth loose in evil (Psalm 50:19) or our behaviour in loose living.

Secondly, remember that Satan also is engaged in binding and loosing wherever he can (1 Thessalonians 2:18, ASB). The outcome therefore depends on who is doing the binding and loosing and what is being bound and loosed. As far as we are concerned we are to—

> Bind what God binds and loose what Satan binds
> Loose what God looses and bind what Satan looses

Thirdly, the two activities often go together. To loose a person from the power of an evil spirit will usually involve binding or restricting the freedom or action of the evil spirit (Mark 1:32-34, 9:25).

Binding or bondages

The detailed analysis of bondages in the New Testament is an indication of the importance of the subject. It also reveals that most of the binding being done is being done by Satan and that the main exercise of our authority is to loose people from their bondages.

1. *The bonds may be literal*
  a. Material shackles or fetters (Luke 8:29).
  b. The condition of imprisonment, captivity or servitude (Philippians 1:7,13; 2 Corinthians 6:7; Matthew 18:26; Titus 2:9).

2. *They may be bodily conditions that restrict a person's freedom of action or expression*
  a. Impediments such as blindness, deafness or speech difficulties (Mark 7:32; Matthew 15:14).
  b. Paralysis or other crippling infirmities (Luke 13:16).

3. *The restraints may be imposed by law*
  a. The purpose of law is to restrain evil in society, and in other areas it sets bounds or limits on individual freedom. For example in marriage law and partnership law (Romans 7:2; 2 Corinthians 6:14).
  b. The law may however be used to restrict the Gospel (Acts 9:1–3).

4. *The bond may be a moral one, that is, the person is restricted in what they feel free to do, not by any outside force but by an inner restraint.* This is important when we come to discuss the nature of the authority we exercise which is mainly a moral and spiritual authority.
  a. A person may bind themselves by a promise or an oath or vow (Acts 20:22f).
  b. Or they may have such a strong inner conviction as to what they should do, that they feel they must do it no matter what the cost (Acts 23:12,21).

c. Conscience functions as an internalised law to restrain our behaviour even in the absence of external law (Romans 2:14).

d. A person may feel 'duty bound', that is bound by a sense of duty or obligation to do something or go somewhere (Romans 1:14).

5. *The bondage may be psychological*

a. Addiction to alcohol, drugs, gambling, etc (1 Timothy 3:8).

b. Slavery to certain moods or emotions such as fear, anxiety, anger, rejection or depression (Proverbs 19:19; Isaiah 54:6; Hebrews 2:14).

c. Domination or manipulation by other people through force of will, personality, emotion or peer pressure.

6. *The bondage may be spiritual*, for example:

a. Sinful habits or sennsuality (Titus 3:22; 2 Peter 2:19).

b. Passivity of mind or will (2 Timothy 2:26). The person is enslaved or captivated and seemingly cannot take any steps towards freedom or see through the deception.

c. Occult bondage (Acts 7:23–24) through involvement in spiritism, witchcraft, magic, pagan religions or societies that are wholly or partly under occult control or involved in occult practices.

d. Demonisation, where the person is under demonic control, either wholly or partly and either temporarily or permanently (Mark 5:1–13).

e. Curses, that is, words of malediction or evil speaking that have become the vehicles for evil spirits to intervene (Luke 6:28; 1 Samuel 17:43).

f. Inner vows that become self-imposed curses or self-fulfilling prophecies because they echo our own inner fears or doubts (Proverbs 26:2).

7. *Circumstances may bind a person so that they have little freedom of action.*

a. Indebtedness or poverty, including the 'poverty trap',

that is, the very poor who need education and skills to get out of their predicament, but lack the money to get training, are unable to move in search of jobs, and have health and nutrition levels that incapacitate them for hard work.

b. Other sets of circumstances sometimes force our hand and leave us few if any options from which to choose.

Who or what are we to bind?

We are to bind on earth whatever the Kingdom of God binds in the heavenlies.

1. *Satan and the demonic hierarchy of powers* (Ephesians 6:12).

Behind the structures of society is the demonic overlay of rulers, authorities, powers and spiritual forces of evil in the unseen, spiritual realm. These are enslaving the human race and interfering with the response of people, institutions and societies to the Gospel (Revelation 20:1–2; Mark 9:25).

a. Geographical, over nations, states, cities, territories and land areas (Daniel 10:13,20; Isaiah 21:9; 1 Kings 11:5; 2 Kings 17:29–31).

b. Over spheres of influence, for example Mammon in relation to money, Moloch in relation to abortion, Aphrodite in relation to sex, etc.

2. *Demons or evil spirits* involved in the demonstration of individuals and groups such as spiritists, covens, adherents of pagan religions and occult societies.

3. *Principalities and powers.* That is the structural manifestations of power in society, governments, bureaucracies, business corporations, national cultures, media, educational institutions, etc.

There is an inner, corporate spirit or persona in these powers that is fallen but not demonic and that is in rebellion against the Lordship of Christ. This rebellion and the actions and influence of the powers are to be restrained where they are in opposition to the Kingdom of God.

4. *The actions, influences and attitudes of people* where they are the instruments of evil or oppression in society. For example pornography, prostitution, abortion, drug traffic, greed and corruption. The powers, in 3 above, are created by people and live and work in and through people.

5. *Circumstances, sickness, conditions and influences* that are in opposition to the will of God, stand in the way of His purposes, hinder the spread of the Gospel or bring suffering and affliction into people's lives.

Who or what are we to loose?

1. *People*, setting them free from their bondages, sicknesses, inhibitions, fears and sins and releasing them to fulfil their God given potential in serving Him. People may need to be set free in their:

a. Human spirit so as to be able to hear from God, worship God and operate effectively in the realm of spiritual gifts and graces.

b. Mind, so that it is freed from compulsive thoughts and renewed by the Holy Spirit.

c. Will, from addictions and enslaving habits.

d. Emotions, from inner hurts, fears and inhibitions.

e. Bodies from physical, psychosomatic and spiritually based sicknesses and disabilities.

f. Relationships, in marriages, families, churches, and social groupings.

2. *Principalities and powers.* The creational or structural powers, that is the organisations and institutions of human societies, which are fallen but not demonic, need to be loosed from the demonic powers so that they are opened up

to change and can be called back to fulfil their God ordained functions and destinies in the Kingdom of God.

We need therefore to:

a. Cast demons out of the structures and out of the geographical or geopolitical spheres in the world.

b. Address the structures of nations and societies with the claims of the Lordship of Jesus Christ.

3. *Resources* of money, facilities, land, equipment, personnel, materials and ideas that are required for the work of the Kingdom of God.

3

First Bind the Strong Man

In Matthew 12 Jesus is involved in a controversy with the Pharisees who claimed he was casting out demons by Beelzebul or Satan, the prince of the demons. In the course of his reply Jesus made this statement:

> *Any kingdom divided against itself is laid waste; and any city or house divided against itself shall not stand. And if Satan casts out Satan, he is divided against himself; how then shall his kingdom stand? And if I by Beelzebul cast out demons, by whom do your sons cast them out? But if I cast out demons by the Spirit of God, then the kingdom of God has come upon you.*
> *Or how can anyone enter the strong man's house and carry off his property, unless he first binds the strong man? And then he will plunder his house.*
> (Matthew 12:25–29, ASB)

In dealing with the matter of binding and loosing, Jesus establishes a very important principle—

First things first—first bind the Strong Man

Many of our common approaches to counselling or problems come at the situation from exactly the opposite approach— first the flesh, then emotional problems, then relational difficulties, then generational ties, and lastly if there is an unexplainable remainder, consider the possibility of demonisation in one form or another.

Jesus says this is like trying to rob a strong man's house while the strong man is still there, and unhampered in his activity.

If demonic strongholds are not dealt with first, the common experience will be that—

1. They will bring confusion and chaos into the process of trying to diagnose what the real problems are. The more you probe, the more entangled and perplexing the matter becomes.
2. They will strongly resist and hinder the attempts of the person to deal with the problems or to open themselves to the grace of God.

Who is the Strong Man?

The New Testament discloses, not a mere principle of evil in the universe, but a highly organised and powerful kingdom, implacably opposed to the will of God and determined to hold man and the world in slavery.

This kingdom of darkness consists of:

1. *Satan, the prince or ruler*
   Satan, the fallen archangel (Ezekiel 28:11–15) is described as the prince or ruler of the demons (Matthew 9:34, 12:24). When Adam fell, he lost his authority over the world, and into the spiritual vacuum that was left Satan came, becoming the god and ruler of this world (John 12:31, 14:30, 16:11; 2 Corinthians 4:4).

   His names reveal his character. Satan, the adversary (1 Peter 5:8), devil, the accuser or slanderer (Revelation 12:10), the evil one (1 John 5:9), the enemy (Luke 10:19), also the deceiver (Revelation 12:10), murderer and the father of lies (John 8:44). He is likened to a serpent (2 Corinthians 11:3), a dragon (Revelation 13:2), and a roaring lion (1 Peter 5:8)!

In his kingdom of darkness, Satan has a throne (Revelation 2:13, 3:2), and fortresses (2 Corinthians 10:4); he has the power to perform signs and wonders (2 Thessalonians 2:9), the power or strength of death (Hebrews 2:14), and deep mysteries of evil (Revelation 2:24; 2 Thessalonians 2:7).

Satan is however neither omnipotent nor omnipresent. He cannot be in more than one place at the same time. He operates through a vast host of fallen angels (2 Peter 2:4; Jude 1:6), spirit beings also called demons (Luke 8:27), evil spirits (Luke 11:26), and unclean spirits (Mark 9:25).

They are organised in—

2. *A hierarchy or structure of evil powers*

This structure is nowhere exhaustively described in Scripture but is referred to in a range of categories and terms. One way of interpreting the rich variety of information is as follows.

Powers that are geopolitical or geographical

a. World rulers (kosmokrator) (Ephesians 6:12) probably the highest order of powers.

b. Principalities (arche) or rulerships, perhaps the gods of the nations or other territories (Daniel 10:13,20; Deuteronomy 32:8–9, RSV, perhaps Acts 16:9).

c. Rulers (archon) (Colossians 1:16; 1 Corinthians 2:6,8) lower orders of geographical or territorial powers, perhaps over specific institutions, etc.

Powers that are over areas or spheres of influence

a. Dominions or lordships (kuriotes). For example, the media, money and wealth (mammon) cultures, academic disciplines, legal systems, etc.

b. Powers (dunamis) (Romans 8:38; Matthew 24:29) including the spiritual force (pneumatikos) of evil in the spiritual realm.

c. Authorities (exousia) (Colossians 2:15; 1 Peter 3:22) beings with the right to use power delegated from the higher orders above them.

The picture is that of a closeknit network of power structures, heavily dependent on one another and on the power of Satan and the world rulers. While Satan is *the* strong man, there will also be in any specific territory, or set of circumstances, or demonised individual, a 'strong man' who represents the power source and the dominating influence in that particular situation. He will be the key to setting the situation free.

Jesus and the Strong Man

When Jesus says, 'First bind the strong man', he is speaking out of a hard won experience. The very first thing that Jesus did after he was baptised and filled with the Holy Spirit was to seek out the strong man, Satan himself, in the wilderness (Matthew 4:1–11).

1. There, in the most unfavourable conditions, the widerness, not a garden like Eden, not freshly rested but after fasting 40 days and nights, he met all the subtlety and deceptive seduction of the fallen archangel, not in one temptation but in three, and came off victorious.

2. Jesus faced Satan, eyeball to eyeball, as a Spirit-filled Man and *established, once and for all, his moral ascendancy over the evil one*. The devil met his match. At the beginning it was the tempter who came to Jesus, at the end it was Jesus who had mastered the tempter and dismissed him peremptorily from his presence. 'Get out of here Satan!'

3. *Satan was bound, that is, his heretofore absolute freedom over the world was now limited, because he knew that if it came to a show-down this Man's will would overmaster his*

every time. Such confrontations he could no longer afford. Henceforth he would have to work indirectly against Jesus, through Peter, through Judas, through the powers, through the elements, to destroy the Man who would thwart him at every turn. That plan was, as we will see, his final undoing.

And plunder his house

After his binding of the strong man in the wilderness, Jesus returned to Galilee in the power of the Spirit (Luke 4:14), came to Nazareth, and in the synagogue declared his manifesto.

> *The Spirit of the Lord is on me, because He has anointed me to preach good news to the poor. He has sent me to proclaim freedom for the prisoners and recovery of sight for the blind, to release the oppressed, to proclaim the year of the Lord's favour.*　　　　(Luke 4:18–19)

His public ministry fulfilled this declaration.

1. *He went around the synagogues, casting out demons.* He forbade the demon to speak, *'Be quiet and come out of him'* (Luke 4:35), commanded a deaf and dumb spirit, *'come out of him and do not enter him again'* (Mark 9:25) and at other times forbidding the demons to speak, because they knew who he was (Mark 1:34). The demons recognised his authority and obeyed him, even seeking his permission before they dared to go into the swine at Gadara (Luke 8:32).

2. *Where evil spirits had afflicted the bodies of men and women he released them. 'This woman, a daughter of Abraham as she is, whom Satan has bound for eighteen long years, should she not have been released from this bond on the sabbath day?'* (Luke 13:16).

3. *In the storm on the lake, Jesus discerned the demonic*

source of the tempest. He rebuked the wind and literally 'muzzled' the sea (Mark 4:39) in exactly the same manner as he dealt with the unclean demon in the synagogue (Luke 4:34).

> *And amazement came upon them all, and they began discussing with one another and saying, 'What is this message? For with authority and power he commands the unclean spirits, and they come out'.* (Luke 4:36)

4. *Having established his unchallenged ascendancy over Satan and the demons, he authorises his disciples to act in his name and likewise to cast out demons* (Luke 9:1–2).

When the seventy disciples come back with joy saying *'Even the demons are subject to us in your name,'* he explained the reason for this,

'I saw Satan fall like lightning from heaven' (Luke 10:17–18). What his disciples had been doing was plundering the strong man's house after the strong man had been bound and inhibited.

5. *The ascendancy and authority that Jesus established over Satan and the demons was declared by him to be through the presence in him of the Holy Spirit and to be evidence of the coming of the Kingdom of God.*

> *But if I drive out demons by the Spirit of God, then the Kingdom of God has come upon you.* (Matthew 12:28)

In other words, Jesus was doing on earth the things that were already being done in heaven.

> *I tell you the truth, the Son can do nothing by himself; he can do only what he sees his Father doing.* (John 5:19)

The victory of the Cross

In 1 Corinthians 2 Paul is speaking of the hidden wisdom in the Cross of Christ,

> *None of the rulers of this age understood it, for if they had they would not have crucified the Lord of glory.*
> (1 Corinthians 2:8)

The rulers of this age, who are coming to nothing (1 Corinthians 2:6) are the Satanic powers who engineered the death of Jesus. What Paul is saying is that if Satan had had any idea of what was going to happen on the Cross, he would have levelled every tree in Palestine rather than let them use one to crucify the Lord of glory. Satan never understood until too late that the Cross was the ultimate and irreversible binding of his power and restriction of his freedom to act.

1. *By his death and his resurrection from the dead, Jesus robbed Satan of his ultimate weapon against the human race.*

> *Since then the children share in flesh and blood, He himself likewise also partook of the same, that through death he might render powerless* (Gk katargeo) *him who had the power of death, that is, the devil; and might deliver those who through fear of death were subject to slavery all their lives.* (Hebrews 2:14–15, ASB)

2. *By his ultimate obedience to death, even death on the Cross (Philippians 2:8) Jesus met and exhausted the rebellion of the principalities and powers,*

> *When he had disarmed* (Gk katargeo) *the rulers and authorities, he made a public display of them having triumphed over them by the Cross.* (Colossians 2:15)

> *Now Jesus has obtained ultimate authority in heaven and*

31

on earth after angels and rulers and authorities and powers have been brought into submission under him.

(1 Peter 3:22)

3. *By the redeeming power of his blood Jesus has delivered us from the authority of darkness and God has transferred us to the kingdom of His beloved Son* (Colossians 1:13). We have been changed from rebellious and disobedient enemies to loving sons and daughters thus robbing Satan, the ruler of the kingdom of the air, the spirit who is now at work in those who are disobedient (Ephesians 2:2) of his ground in our lives.

4. *The work of Jesus in dispossessing Satan of his hold on mankind is to be carried on in this age by his followers, exercising his authority in his name by the power of his Spirit.*

The reason the Son of God appeared was to destroy (literally, 'loose') the devil's work (1 John 3:8).

> *Truly, truly, I say to you, he who believes in me, the works that I do shall he do also; and greater works than these shall he do; because I go to the Father.*
>
> (John 14:12, ASB)

> *Behold I have given you authority to tread on serpents and scorpions, and over all the power of the enemy, and nothing shall injure you.* (Luke 10:19, ASB)

4

How to Bind the Strong Man

When it comes to binding the strong man, Jesus does not
leave us with only vague ideas about what is meant. In Luke
11 he goes into very precise detail as to what it means and
how it is to be done.

> *When a strong man, fully armed, guards his own house,
> his possessions are safe. But when someone stronger
> attacks and overpowers him, he takes away the armour
> in which the man trusted and divides up the spoils.*
>
> (Luke 11:21)

Here are the important steps that are involved.

1. Identify the strong man

In every place or set of circumstances, or even in an individual life, there will be a demonic power that controls the
situation, organises the defence and is the primary source of
power or energy for other spirits that may be involved. Some
indicators as to the identity of the strong man are:

a. The armour (panopleia) he is wearing
The word panopleia is used only twice in the New Testa-
ment. In Ephesians 6:12–18 it refers to the full armour of
God and in Luke 11:21 it refers to the full armour of Satan.

The full armour of God is a set of life conditions that God wants to establish in our life which will enable God to work in us and will prevent or restrict Satan working in us.

The full armour of Satan is a set of life conditions that Satan wants to establish in our life which will allow him to work in us and will prevent or restrict God from working in us.

The life conditions of Satan will be the reverse of the life conditions God wants to establish.

The full armour of God	The full armour of Satan
Truth	Lies, deception
Peace	Strife, contention
Righteousness (right relatedness)	Alienation, rejection
Faith	Mistrust, suspicion, doubt
Hope	Despair, depression
The Word of God	Human reasoning
Prayer	Occultic meditation

If we can identify the major components of the life conditions in the individual or the institution we may be able to work back from them to identify the character of the strong man.

b. The state of the 'house'
When demons enter and dwell in a person, it is called their 'house' (Luke 11:24–26). The same is true of an institution or a geopolitical entity such as a city. What is implied is that there is some correspondence between the state or condition of the 'house' and the nature of its occupants. Thus scripture identifies a deaf and dumb spirit (Mark 9:25), an unclean spirit (Luke 4:33), a spirit of divination (Acts 16:16), and so on.

c. The name
In Scripture a name always indicates an identity or a character. For this reason the name of the strong man is sometimes

34

the key to taking effective action against him and on occasions you find Jesus demanding the name of the demon in control of other demons. This is clearly the case with the Gadarene demoniac. Jesus treats the spirit as an individual, *'Come out of the man you unclean spirit'* (Mark 5:8) and it speaks in the singular, *'What have you to do with me?'*... *'do not torment me'*... *'my name is Legion'* (vs 6,9). Then it is the demons (plural) who beg Jesus not to send them out of the area. Jesus gave them permission to enter the swine, and the evil spirits came out of the man and into the animals (vs 12–13). Legion was the name of the strong man who controlled and empowered the host of other demons in the man.

Note, however, that Jesus did not always ask for the name, although it is clear he always knew the nature of the spirits he was dealing with.

The nature of the demonic strong man may also be revealed through the spiritual gifts of a word of knowledge or the discernment of spirits.

2. Get more power on your side than the strong man has

In Ephesians 6:10–18 Paul emphasises what Jesus also asserts, that engaging and overcoming the strong man is by no means a pushover. It is neither metaphorical war or make believe war, it is real war, therefore the passage is full of strong imperatives like 'struggle', 'withstand', 'be strong', 'keep alert', 'the evil day', and so on.

Our strength lies in our confidence in the absolute victory of the death and resurrection of Christ over Satan and all his hosts, and our personal relationship with the Victor himself. It also rests in the certainty of the authority that has been given to us to preach the Gospel, heal the sick and cast out demons.

But we still need the full armour of God—that is the life conditions that enable us to overcome. But life conditions require appropriation and obedience to take effect, therefore our capacity for the task of binding a particular strong man always has a relativity about it. We may find that we are tackling more than we can manage on our own, therefore we must never hesitate to call in help. In fact, warfare is always a corporate activity and victory goes to the side that can muster superior strength (Ephesians 6:10; Romans 13:12–14).

3. Get on the attack

One of the common manifestations of demonic control is the passivity that is induced; the person's will is inert, the mind is dull and the spirit is torpid and lifeless. From the strong man's perspective, everything is undisturbed and at peace. The perils of passivity from our point of view, however, is that it gives all the initiative over to Satan and loses the battle by default.

Even defence is inadequate—that is, fight only when you are attacked. Defence at best only prevents defeat, it will never win a war. The Biblical principle is always attack, which is why the Bible gives no instructions for fortifying a defensive position. Joshua goes out to fight Amalek, David runs out to meet Goliath, and Jesus goes out into the wilderness to encounter Satan.

Attack seizes the initiative from the enemy, dictates the terms of battle and chooses the ground on which it will be fought. The grounds of our victory are the grounds of Calvary.

> For the accuser of our brethren who accuses them before our God day and night, has been hurled down. They overcame him by the blood of the Lamb and by the word of their testimony. (Revelation 12:10–11)

The strong man's position is vulnerable, but it is vulnerable only to attack.

4. Overpower him

The attack must be pressed until the strong man is overpowered. Even in the ministry of Jesus it seems that deliverance was not always an instantaneous thing, there was resistance and arguing and sometimes the action of Jesus is in the continuous, *'He had been saying to him "Come out of the man you unclean spirit"'* (Mark 5:8).

We will discuss more fully later the nature of the power that is involved in binding and loosing, but here we need to emphasise that ultimate victory comes by insisting that God's will be done on earth as it is in heaven. We need to persist in that stance until resistance crumbles, as ultimately it must.

5. Take away the armour in which the man trusted

That means dealing with the life conditions that have enabled the strong man to maintain his position. When the strong man is bound, and often only after the strong man is bound, we can get access to the specific life problems that need to be dealt with. This is critical in order to dismantle the demonic strongholds (2 Corinthians 10:4) and to set the person free. It will involve:

a. *Freeing the person's will* so that it can make wholehearted choices for Christ against Satan and satanic bondages. No matter how buried the person's will is, there remains the freedom of moral choice that God always protects.

b. *Dealing one by one with sins, enslaving habits, occult*

bondages, fears and other problems. Often there will be a tangle that has to be carefully unpicked.

c. *Repentance, forgiveness, cleansing and the re-ordering of the person's thought patterns and lifestyle*, replacing the demonic life conditions with the armour of God, the life conditions that God wants to establish.

As the strongholds are broken down and the life conditions are changed there may well be successive deliverances from evil spirits associated with these states. Cut off from the power of the strong man however, they can generally be dealt with very easily, or they may leave of their own accord.

6. Divide up the spoils

The purpose of binding is to loose. Getting rid of demonic control and infestation is the negative aspect, releasing the life into the fulness of its potential is the positive side, that is loosing.

A person's problems are almost always a pointer to their best potential because Satan will try to spoil a life along the line of its greatest strengths. We need to release life and creativity into those atrophied areas that have been denied expression so that the person can begin to become all that God created them to be. That is enjoying the spoils of war in a spiritual sense.

5

Binding and Loosing—the Word of God and the Authority of the Believer

Before we can effectively bind anybody or anything, or for that matter loose or release anyone who is bound, we have to know how the process works and what we are actually dealing with. Otherwise we will fall into the trap of thinking that all we have done is to recite the correct formula and things will happen. We soon discover that nothing happens, no matter how loud we shout or what words we use.

For our present purpose we can ignore physical chains or imprisonment because you cannot chain a demon or put an evil spirit in a prison cell. We therefore have to consider the ways in which a person's freedom can be taken away or restricted without the use of actual physical force. There are three means that are relevant,

1. Law
2. Authority
3. Spiritual power

The force of law

Law has the power to restrict our freedom of action in anything it orders us to do or in anything it prohibits us from doing. Law does not ask for our agreement with its demands, nor does it consult our preferences, or priorities. It claims that we 'ought' to do what it says, whether we like it or not, and it is prepared, if necessary, to penalise or punish infractions in order to enforce its commands.

We may readily obey the requirements of the law because we agree with them as being good law and consider that everybody else should also obey. In that case there is no sense of restriction on our freedom, because we freely choose to do the things that the law requires. We are not conscious of the law having any binding effect on us because we obey it willingly. That is the way in which we, as Christians, have been enabled to live in the freedom of obedience to the law of God.

In other cases, however, we obey the law, in the sense of complying with its demands, but we do so only because we do not want to be penalised or punished for breaking the law. Our freedom, in other words, is limited or restricted by the coercive power wielded by the law.

When we make a promise or a vow to do something, or not to do something, our freedom of choice or action is also restricted by that promise because we feel 'bound' in conscience to keep our word. The force of conscience is like that of an internalised law, but it has positive responses as well as negative ones. In this it differs from external law which does not reward us for keeping its commands but only penalises us if we do not. On the other hand, conscience commends us when we do what it approves (1 Peter 3:16; Acts 24:16)—we have a 'good conscience' about it. But like the law, conscience penalises us if we disobey it, it accuses us (Romans 2:15), and lets us experience unpleasant feelings of guilt and failure.

Satan and the Word of God

Satan is bound, that is, his freedom of action, and the freedom of the demons is restricted when they are confronted with the Word of God. Sometimes it is said that

40

Satan is a legalist, but it is not that he respects the law, he fears the Lawgiver. That was the dreadful, crippling effect on him of the words of Jesus, *'It is written...'* (Luke 4:4). James describes the reaction of the demons likewise,

> *You believe that there is one God. Good! Even the demons believe that—and shudder.* (James 2:19)

One of the primary means of binding Satan and the demons is by the use of the Word of God, the sword of the Spirit (Ephesians 6:17).

1. *The Word of God is an entity containing divine power to accomplish itself.* Thus the judgement word possesses and releases its own power to produce what it proclaims.

2. *The Word of God, once spoken, has a history of its own, it remains alive and powerful in succeeding generations and different situations.*

> *So is my word that goes out from my mouth: It will not return to me empty, but will accomplish what I desire and achieve the purpose for which I sent it.*
> (Isaiah 55:11)

3. *The demons know that every act of disobedience or resistance on their part increases their dread of the Lord who is watching over his word to perform it or to see it fulfilled* (Jeremiah 1:12). When their fear becomes unbearable they give way to the Word of God.

> *'Be quiet!'* said Jesus sternly, *'Come out of him!'* The evil spirit shook the man violently and came out of him with a shriek. (Mark 1:26)

The effect of authority

We need to distinguish very carefully between power (dunamis) and authority (exousia).

Power is the strength or potency to get done whatever you will to do even in the face of opposition or dysfunctional circumstances. In this sense, all power belongs to God.

> *Once God has spoken*
> *Twice I have heard this:*
> *That power belongs to God.*   (Psalm 62:11, ASB)

Authority is the delegated right to exercise the prerogatives of power, or to represent the power of one whose will and commands must be obeyed by others.

Authority stands in relation to power in much the same way as law stands in relation to the state with its police and its armed forces. Authority acts on behalf of power, but it seeks and expects to obtain the desired results without having to call on the use of coercive power. In the ultimate, however, we obey authority because we recognise that either:

1. The authority figure also has the power to enforce obedience or punish disobedience, or

2. It can call on the source of its authority and that power source will enforce obedience to the authority or punish disobedience.

Authority therefore *exercises the right or power to command,* and *Power enforces the commands of authority.*

The authority of the believer and the demons

The distinction between power and authority is important for understanding the authority of the believer over the demons. *Sometimes the believer is meant to move in power, but always he is meant to move in authority.*

The authority of the believer to represent the power of God in relation to Satan and the demons is dependent on the following conditions.

1. **Obedience.** The believer must be living in obedience to the source of his power, that is, to Christ. Like the Roman centurion who so impressed Jesus, he must be a man 'under authority'.

> *But just say the word and my servant will be healed. For I myself am a man under authority, with soldiers under me. I tell this one, 'Go' and he goes; and that one, 'Come' and he comes, I say to my servant, 'Do this' and he does it.* (Matthew 8:8–9)

The centurion's men obeyed him without question because they knew that if they disobeyed the centurion, the centurion's superior officer would back him up and *his* superior officer would back him up, all the way back to Caesar on his throne in Rome. All the power of the Roman Empire stood behind the centurion—as long as he stayed under authority. If he stepped out of that obedience he would have no authority at all.

The authority of the believer therefore depends on two factors: one is the power and authority that belongs to Christ as Head of the Church; the other is our relationship to him, and that relationship is obedience.

2. **A knowledge of the extent of his authority**, that is, what he can do and command and what things are beyond the scope of his rights in this regard.

The authority of Christ is absolute, all authority in heaven and on earth, spiritual and temporal (Matthew 28:18). As Head of the Church he has delegated authority to his Body,
    a. *Over sickness and demons*

43

He gave them authority over unclean spirits, to cast them out, and to heal every kind of disease and every kind of sickness. (Matthew 10:1)

b. *Over all of Satan's ability*

Behold I have given you authority to tread on serpents and scorpions, and over all the power of the enemy, and nothing shall injure you. (Luke 10:19)

Of one thing you can be certain, the demons know whether we are sure of our grounds or unsure, and whether we are within the scope of our rightful authority or have exceeded it.

3. A growing knowledge of the character and the ways and purposes of God who is the source of his authority.

What gave Jesus such authority on earth was his total identification with the will and purposes of his Father in heaven.

The Son can do nothing by himself; he can do only what he sees the Father doing, because whatever the Father does, the Son also does. (John 5:19)

My Father is always at his work to this very day and I too am working. (John 5:17)

I do nothing on my own but speak just what the Father has taught me. The one who sent me is with me; he has not left me alone, for I always do what pleases him. (John 8:28–29)

Just as the Father sent the Son into the world to live and act on his behalf, to do his will on earth as it is done in heaven, so Christ has sent us. '*As you sent me into the world, I have sent them into the world*' (John 17:18). We are to do the same as Jesus did, to do the will of the One who has sent

44

us, that is, to do on earth the things that are in harmony with his deeds in heaven.

It is for this reason that Scripture has given us such a mass of information on the way in which Jesus lived and thought and acted. His life is told four times over in the Gospels, one third of the entire New Testament. We need a continuous and continual revelation of his character and his works, the 'seeing' that Jesus spoke about in John 5:19.

4. Confidence to act on his authority

This is the critical point because authority is not authority unless it is used. If we know our grounds and know the kind of decisions and responses that are appropriate, then we have to act. Specifically we need,

a. *The confidence to act or decide, or command.*

b. *Confidence in the decisions we make or the commands we give,* and

c. *Confidence that Christ will back us up and, if necessary, enforce our commands or decisions.*

It is here that our will becomes important. In binding the activity of the demons, or releasing their hold on people, we have to hold the commands we give in the name or authority of Christ, with our will against the will of the demons. And we have to hold that pressure against them until resistance crumbles. God's will is done by God willing it in heaven and man willing it on earth, actively insisting at all costs, *'Thy will be done on earth as it is in heaven.'*

In other words, the force of authority is moral pressure. The person exercising it makes the other person feel uneasy and threatened if they resist so that eventually they give way in order to get release from the pressure. That is the pressure that commands truly given in the authority of Jesus Christ put on the demons.

The pressure is increased when the person exercising authority is confident of their position and confident of the final outcome of the conflict and the person resisting is unsure of themselves and of their ability to successfully resist. The

Prussian General, Clauswitz, wrote in his principles of warfare that it is more important to destroy the courage of the enemy's troops than to destroy his troops. The same principles hold true in spiritual warfare. Praise, worship, the proclamation of Scripture and the rehearsing of the works of God not only encourage our confidence in victory, they devastate the morale and will to resist of the evil spirits.

Authority and the Name of Jesus

Authority is vested in the Name of Jesus.

> *God exalted him to the highest place and gave him the name that is above every name, that at the name of Jesus every knee should bow, in heaven and on earth and under the earth, and every tongue confess that Jesus Christ is Lord, to the glory of God the Father.*
>
> (Philippians 2:10–11)

Authority is in the Name, power is in the Spirit. When the disciples were sent out by Jesus and given authority over the demons, they reported, *'Lord, even the demons submit to us in your name.'* The signs that were promised to accompany those who believe were

> *In my name they will drive out demons; they will speak with new tongues: they will pick up snakes with their hands; and when they drink deadly poison it will not hurt them at all; they will place their hands on sick people and they will get well.* (Mark 16:17–18)

The Name of Jesus sums up all he is in his victory, his standing, his office as Prophet, Priest and King, his exaltation and his eternal glory. All authority in heaven and on earth has been given to him (Matthew 28:18). When we

46

speak or act in his Name, we represent him, therefore we are to do the works that he did, in the same spirit that he did and with the same end, to glorify the Father.

Christ has unlimited authority, even infinite authority. We do not have authority to that extent, but to the extent that he has given us authority we are to use it, not to say but to do. It is not a matter of merely saying 'In the Name of Jesus' it is seeing that God's will is done on earth as it is in heaven by,

Understanding his will, both the general and the specific

Obeying his will

Embodying his will, and

Doing his will, that is, *willing* his will

The will of the believer, humbly and obediently resting in the divine will, and actively willing that will against the powers of darkness is what puts demons to flight. Their fear is, that if they resist too long they will face the power of a holy God who will come to enforce the commands of his servants.

It is to the power aspect of binding and loosing that we will turn in the next chapter.

6

Binding and Loosing and
the Power of the Holy Spirit

We have seen that authority rests on power, and that authority without the power to back up its commands is helpless. On the other hand, where authority is accompanied by access to adequate power it need not necessarily use that power. It is capable of producing results solely by the moral weight and influence that power gives to its commands.

As far as the authority of the believer is concerned, including that of binding and loosing, the power that backs up and validates that authority is the power of the Holy Spirit. He is the One who dwells in us (1 Corinthians 3:16), and has made us competent as ministers of the new covenant (2 Corinthians 3:6). The power gifts that are meant to mark the ministry of the church are manifestations of his presence (1 Corinthians 12:4–10). We still have to ask, however,

1. What is meant by the power of the Holy Spirit?
2. What kind of power is it?
3. How are we meant to gain access to that power?

The Holy Spirit and power

Spirit and power are linked together with unfailing regularity throughout the whole of Scripture, and particularly when we turn to the Gospel record of the life of Jesus.

He was conceived when the power of the Spirit overshadowed the Virgin Mary (Luke 1:35) and his public ministry began when the Holy Spirit came upon him after his baptism (Mark 1:10). He was sent by the Spirit into the desert to face the strong man, Satan (Mark 1:12–13) and returned from that victory in the power of the Spirit (Luke 4:14).

It was the Holy Spirit whose anointing consecrated Jesus as the Messiah, the Lord's Anointed King, and who empowered him to preach good news to the poor, freedom for prisoners and release for the oppressed (Luke 4:18). Henceforth everything he did, he did as a man filled with the Holy Spirit. He healed by the power of the Holy Spirit (Acts 10:38), and when he cast out demons he did it by the Spirit of God (Matthew 12:28).

After the resurrection, the disciples also were told to wait in the city until they were *'clothed with power from on high'* (Luke 24:49) and that they would receive that power when the Holy Spirit came upon them (Acts 1:8). Throughout the history of the early church the same linking of Spirit and power is maintained. When the gathered church prayed for God to stretch out His hand to heal and to perform miraculous signs and wonders, the place where they were meeting was shaken and they were all filled with the Holy Spirit (Acts 4:30–31).

Henceforth the apostolic preaching is not simply with words, but also with power, with the Holy Spirit (1 Thessalonians 1:5), and signs and miracles represent the demonstration of the Spirit's power (Romans 15:19; 1 Corinthians 2:5).

The nature of the Spirit's power

The Greek word for power, dunamis, is the root of our English word dynamite, but the power of the Holy Spirit is not to be thought of in those terms. It is not some kind of energy flow or force field.

The Holy Spirit who is the power of the Lord, is a person, therefore his power is the power of personal presence.

Where the Holy Spirit is, the power of the Lord is present, and where the power of the Lord is manifested, it is because the Holy Spirit is present.

Note the following important points.

1. *The presence of God is not the same on every occasion or in every place. Firstly, there is a structural or general presence of the Holy Spirit in creation.* In him we live and move and have our being (Acts 17:28).

> *Where can I go from your Spirit?*
> *Where can I flee from your presence?*
> *If I go up to the heavens, you are there;*
> *If I make my bed in the depths, you are there.*
> *If I rise on the wings of the dawn,*
> *if I settle on the far side of the sea,*
> *Even there your hand will guide me,*
> *Your right hand will hold me fast*   (Psalm 139:7–10).

This structural presence of God undergirds all forms of more specific manifestations of His presence amongst His people.

2. *Secondly, the Holy Spirit is especially present at certain times, and especially present in certain places. These occasions are to be understood as a greater intensification of His presence.* Even in the ministry of Jesus such experiences of the manifestation of the Holy Spirit's presence seem to have been variable. For example, the Holy Spirit who came upon him as a dove at his baptism, was also the cloud that enveloped him on the Mount of Transfiguration (Mark 9:7). He was the power of the Lord that was present for Jesus to perform healing (Luke 5:17), and that was coming from him and healing those who touched him (Luke 6:19, 8:46). These occasions are specially noted, but Jesus, who had the Spirit

without measure, always moved in authority, whether the specific manifestation of the Spirit's presence was observable or not.

3. *Our experience of the Holy Spirit's presence will follow that of Jesus.* The Spirit is the anointing that we have received, and he abides (1 John 2:27), because we are indwelt by his presence (1 Corinthians 3:16). But we will experience the power of the Holy Spirit in a special measure from time to time. On those occasions there is an intensified presence of the Spirit within us or amongst us. In different terminology it is the difference between being full of the Holy Spirit which is meant to be our continual experience (Luke 4:1) and being filled with the Spirit for a particular purpose (Acts 4:8).

4. *The nature of the Holy Spirit's power, as that of personal presence, also governs its character.* Thus He is,

a. *The Spirit of glory* (1 Peter 4:14). Glory is God's majesty and power, and power and glory interpenetrate one another (Ephesians 3:16; Colossians 1:11; Revelation 15:8).

b. *The Spirit of holiness* (Romans 1:4). Holiness is God's unique dignity, He alone is holy (1 Samuel 2:2). Holy and awesome is His name (Psalm 111:9).

c. *The Spirit of love* (Romans 5:5) who unites us to himself so that nothing will ever separate us from the love of Christ (Romans 8:38–39) and intercedes for us 'with groans that words cannot express' (Romans 8:26).

d. *The Spirit of grace* (Hebrews 10:29) expressed in forgiveness, kindness, acceptance and magnanimity towards the undeserving.

e. *The Spirit of life* (Romans 8:1) creative, redemptive and death swallowing.

All these, and many other manifestations of the Spirit's power constitute the moral and spiritual splendour of God's presence that will overthrow Satan and all his hosts (2 Thessalonians 2:8) because no evil can stand before His holiness. In Jesus' person it caused the demons to cry out in fear *'What have you to do with us, O Son of God? Have you come here to torment us before the time?'* (Matthew 8:29).

How do we gain access to the Holy Spirit's power?

Because the power of the Holy Spirit is the power of personal presence, we are dealing with those special intensifications of his presence that seem to take place at particular times and on particular occasions. Regarding them we can make the following observations:

1. *The intensification of the Holy Spirit's presence can be affected by the part played by man.*
   a. *It is adversely affected by man's sin and rebellion* (Jeremiah 23:29; Psalm 51:11; Isaiah 63:10). God has given up the use of coercive power to protect the integrity of the relationship He desires with man.
   b. *It is positively affected by human receptivity and human need* (Acts 10:44; Isaiah 61:1f), *and the openness of the situation.*

2. *We are able to experience such intensifications of the Holy Spirit's presence,* but not to produce them. Nevertheless we can, and should ask for them and seek them (Exodus 33:15; Acts 4:29–31).

3. *The intensifications of divine presence seem to have these characteristics:*
   a. *They are temporary,*
   b. *They are initiated by God,* that is there is a certain sovereignty about them (Joel 2:28), and,
   c. *They are effective* (Romans 15:18–19).
   Nevertheless there remains the possibility of disbelief or rejection, they do not compel faith (Matthew 12:38–39).

Openness to the Holy Spirit's presence

Although there is a sovereignty about the special intensifications of the Holy Spirit's presence, it is his desire to be present in such ways with us. The openness and receptivity that can enable him to be present amongst us is developed in the following ways:

1. *Through the baptism in the Holy Spirit.* Power, which means presence, is the promised result of the baptism in the Holy Spirit (Acts 1:8, 2:1–4, etc). The Holy Spirit is the Angel or Messenger of God's Presence (Isaiah 63:11).

2. *Through the operation of the gifts of the Holy Spirit* (1 Corinthians 12:7–10). The gifts are described as manifestations of the Spirit, that is, personal communications by him or special enablings or capacities bestowed by his intensified presence in us.

3. *Through prayer and intercession.* Prayer in the life of Jesus was the key to his experience of the Spirit's presence and power (cf Luke 6:12 with Luke 6:19). Intercession by the church in Acts 4:23–31 was answered by a dramatic experience of the Holy Spirit's presence.

4. *Through praise and worship.* Like intercession, worship opens up our lives to the divine presence. He inhabits the praises of Israel (Psalm 22:3 marg., ASB).

5. *Through an attitude of expectancy.* Receptivity to the presence of the Holy Spirit must be cultivated as a continual attitude of heart. God answers our expectations, and none more so than the Holy Spirit who dwells in our body as his temple. The Holy Spirit is no less than God localised in us, seeking our fellowship and our communion. Note the importance of praying in the Spirit (Jude 20; 1 Corinthians 14:2, 14–15).

The importance of the Holy Spirit in binding and loosing

All that we have dealt with in this study arises from *God's intention to share His power with mankind so that man can cooperate with Him in achieving His goals for creation.* But through the fall, man has been set on a course of misusing the power given to him and with the existence of Satan and the evil spirits there is a power clash in the universe.

Nevertheless, for the sake of the integrity of the relationship God desires with man, he has laid aside the use of coercive power; His power is with man and for man rather than control over man. His intention is unchanged, that redeemed man should effect His will on earth as it is done in heaven. His presence and His power are to enable this to be done by working with man and through man.

The intensified presence of the Holy Spirit is of vital importance for the exercise of our authority to bind and loose, in the following ways.

1. *To give us revelation as to the extent of our authority and what has been given us.*

> *Now we have received, not the spirit of the world but the Spirit who is from God that we might know the things freely given to us by God.* (1 Corinthians 2:12)

2. *To give us revelation regarding the character and ways and purposes of God.*

> *For who among men knows the thoughts of a man except the spirit of the man which is in him. Even so the thoughts of God no one knows except the Spirit of God.* (1 Corinthians 2:11)

3. *To give us discernment and knowledge as to the nature of the demonic strong man or strongholds we are facing.* This

may come through the spiritual gifts of a word of knowledge, a word of wisdom, or the discerning of spirits.

4. *To guide us in the use of Scripture, the 'sword of the Spirit' against the demons* (Ephesians 6:17), particularly the rhema word, the specific Spirit-quickened word.

5. *Where the word of authority does not produce a decisive result, then for the gift of miracles to effect deliverance and the gift of healing if necessary, to bind up any damage that the person has suffered.*

6. *That we ourselves may be continuously strengthened in the inner man* (Ephesians 3:16) so as not to be affected by the battle.